Calling the Wild

Calling the Wild

Robert Hilles

Black Moss Press
Settlements Series
2005

Library and Archives Canada Cataloguing in Publication

Hilles, Robert, 1951-
    Calling the wild / Robert Hilles.

(Settlement series ; 2)
ISBN 0-88753-411-2

    1. Hilles, Robert, 1951-. 2. Authors, Canadian (English)–
20th century–Biography. I. Title. II. Series.

PS8565.I48Z463 2005   C811'.54   C2005-906051-4

Published by Black Moss Press at 2450 Byng Road, Windsor, Ontario N8W 3E8.

This is the second in a series called SETTLEMENTS, a series that focuses upon neighbourhoods and regions in Canada.

Black Moss gratefully acknowledges the generous support given by the Canada Council for the Arts and the Ontario Arts Council for its publishing program.

Le Conseil des Arts | The Canada Council
du Canada | for the Arts

ONTARIO ARTS COUNCIL
CONSEIL DES ARTS DE L'ONTARIO

For Pearl, Mickey, Hazel, Brian, and Cathi.

And special thanks to John B. Lee for the editing,
to Marty Gervais for continuing to believe in my work,
and to Peter Levitt for pointing the way.

table of contents

My father and George Smith duck hunting
behind the Smith farm, likely in 1940

Preface

AM CALLING the wild from where it is lost deep in the darkly forested regions of my childhood. I was born and came of age in the Precambrian shield of Northwestern Ontario, mountain country with peaks much older than the Rockies worn down to low granite tree-lined ridges. Perhaps, in a few millions years those rocky hills will be reduced finally to rolling regions, easing into flat lands, becoming mere islands again surrounded by Lake Agassiz—that massive lake, which twelve thousand years ago spanned an area from here to the inland borders of Saskatchewan. From this place here. From this very place. From this place as it was in the time of my childhood—I'm calling the wild. The wild does not reply.

I grew up in the small community of Longbow Lake, which is on the Transcanada Highway and eighteen kilometers east of Kenora, a mill town located on the northern shore of Lake of the Woods—a watery remains of the southeastern tip of Lake Agassiz.

In the nearly three centuries, since La Verendrye first passed this way in search of the Northwest Passage, this region has served many masters: fur traders, railway barons, and paper mill moguls. Originally named Rat Portage, the town was renamed to Kenora in 1905.

Through it all, there have been tourists. Many of them come to hunt and fish because this is game country. Or was. In recent decades tourists in floatplanes, helicopters, 4X4s, and snowmobiles have killed most of the game. When I was a teenager in the 1960s, I could canoe from Dogtooth Lake to East Hawk Lake without seeing another human, but not anymore. During a recent trip, I discovered that what I thought of as backcountry is now laced with fresh gravel roads each leading to a granite-faced shoreline.

Although there are plenty of cottages and resorts, we never thought of this area as cottage country—that was someplace in genteel southern Ontario.

Instead, this is remote, challenging, and yes, wild territory with numerous unnamed lakes surrounded by stands of poplar, spruce, and pine. It is still possible to step into the bush to pee and never be heard from again.

However, if I were to drive south to Rushing River or boat across Dogtooth Lake, a satellite dish would adorn each house I pass. When I was a boy, we didn't have TV until 1959, and even then, the tallest TV antennas only picked up a snowy signal from the CBC station in Winnipeg or nothing at all.

Aerial photographs reveal that this area is comprised more of water than land giving the illusion from the air of a large island-filled lake. On the ground, the trees and hills obscure much of that water because few lakes span more than a mile and most are surrounded by swamps, marshes or thickly wooded hills.

It's the lakes that bring the tourists. Smartly printed Government-of-Ontario brochures now advertise Kenora as *Sunset Country*. A marketing, romantic-sounding phrase likely dreamed up in Toronto, by people who never set foot here.

Still every summer the tourists come, many drawn by those brochures of a world untouched by time, where hunting and fishing hasn't changed from the days of the fur traders, or maybe even before that when First Nation's hunters Ojibway, Assiniboine, and Cree fought the Sioux invaders from the south. Names like Sioux Lookout and Sioux Narrows bear witness to that time.

Before them, around a 1000 A.D. this area was home to the Laurel and Blackduck peoples. Archeologists have found evidence of hunters on the shores of Lake of Woods as far back as 2000 B.C. when the present shorelines became set.

Now, floatplanes fly tourists to remote lakes where they sleep in comfortable cabins and take leisurely walks mindful to carry a handheld GPS device and cell phone with them in case they get lost. They accompany guides who lead them through the backcountry to a scenic spot to sit and wait as hired help seek out and scare up trophy animals. If my father were still alive, he would scoff at this kind of hunting and consider it undignified. Killing for the sake of killing, not for survival, not for a winter's supply of meat. This is the gentry's version of hunting more akin to the foxhunt.

Some would say that my father was a drunk; my mother was a mad woman, and that we, their three children, were wastrels growing wild. But this was my family. This was my story. To others the man who raised me was a loser living on the boundaries of civilization. A three pack a day outsider wasting his life on cheap beer, bad TV and roll-your-own smokes. We lived on the outer edges of a disappearing wilderness.

My father was born in Kenora in 1920 and raised by Royal and Alice Smith on a farm at Longbow Lake. Royal Smith was a distant cousin of my grandmother. My father never knew his mother nor did he know that he was related to Royal. All he knew was that he was the son of Estella Hill, an unwed mother who gave him up not long after he was born. She named him Austen Edwin Hilles, but he was given the nickname Mickey and went by the name Mickey Smith until the war. When I was a boy, many people still called him that.

My mother was born in Dryden in 1926 and met my father when she cleaned cabins at Redden's Camp on Longbow Lake. Her maiden name was Hazel McLean Holmes.

My parents married in 1951, shortly before my birth and two years later my brother Brian was born and in 1958 my sister Catherine Ann.

My father built our first house at Longbow Lake. It took him five years and we lived there from 1957 until March 1964, when it burned down. Fortunately, no one was at home at the time of the fire, though a dog and cat perished in it. The house had two bedrooms. My parents slept in one and us three children shared the other. In the living room, we stoked a large, cast-iron heater all winter. Across from it was the walnut radio that was replaced by a black and white RCA TV in 1959. Along the varnished pine wall that separated the kitchen from the living room was a green couch and across from it, a red chair my father always sat in to watch TV. In the kitchen, there was a ringer washer near the front door and a wood stove against a far wall filled with windows. We ate most of our meals at the rectangle metal table in the middle of the room. Even at the time of the fire, the house wasn't finished. Cupboards lacked doors, there was no running water, and the septic system was still just a hole in the ground.

Our nearest neighbours were Royal and Alice who still lived on the farm where my father grew up. That farm was a half-mile east of us and its south fence ran along the Transcanada.

After our house burned, we rented a house near the junction of the Transcanada Highway (Highway 17) and The Great River Road (Highway 71). I was never certain if the Department of Highways intended those highway numbers to be mirror images of each other or if that was one of life's happy coincidences. The one spanned the whole of Canada while the other went straight south to the Gulf of Mexico.

The house we rented belonged to the Campbell family in Winnipeg and had been previously rented by the Bellamy family. Like everyone in town, we called it the Bellamy house. They had two boys neither of whom did particularly well in school. The only contact my brother and I had with them was a hockey game we played against them on Longbow Lake. We cleared the bay across the highway from the Bellamy house and both fathers played goal while the opposing sons tried to score on them. Our family won. Not long afterward, they moved away. The house sat empty until we moved there.

My parents lived in that house until my father retired in 1985. They then moved to Winnipeg.

For the first sixty-five years of my father's life, he rarely ventured far from Longbow Lake. But after 1985, he hardly set eyes on it.

Longbow Lake is a narrow lake, barely a mile wide, but seven miles long. Its western tip empties into Lake of the Woods at the Blindfold dam. Often in the book when I mention *the lake* I mean Longbow Lake. During the first eighteen years of my life, that lake was an important focal point for me too.

What I've collected in this book are some of the stories from that time and place. But I've also included several of my father's stories all of them contemplating the wild in and around us.

My father with Royal and Alice Smith in the field behind the Smith house sometime between 1940 and 1942

Chickadee

I was about ten, the first time my father told this story to my brother and me. We were in bed while he sat in an oak chair he'd found in the dump and my mother put in our bedroom. I've tried to tell this story the way my father did. Not exactly in his voice, but a close approximation. My father began most of his stories the same way. "Have you heard the one about..." and so it goes.

HAVE YOU heard the one about Chickadee Brant? He got the nickname Chickadee supposedly because during the depression his family survived by eating chickadees.

Late one fall, in early November, a dozen wolves cornered Chickadee. He killed all of them except one and that was his mistake. When it comes to wild animals, especially wolves that travel in packs, it's best to let them be, give them a wide berth. But if you kill one, you had better kill them all.

When you hunt in the bush, you need to listen to your body not your head. Some people believe it's the mind's job to do all the thinking. But without the body's help the brain wouldn't know if it were floating in a lake or standing in a kitchen.

He'd hunted since he was eight, so that makes what happened even more strange. Hunters, good ones like Chickadee, rarely make mistakes.

He was a big man with hands that could circle the barrel of a double-gauge shotgun and still have finger left. He had the strength to strangle a male white-tailed deer and did at least once that I know of carrying the carcass four miles through dense bush to the nearest road. He split the meat with the man who gave him a lift into town.

Chickadee had a wife and five kids, but between his thirty-ninth and fortieth birthday they left. One morning, most likely when Chickadee was at work, Geraldine loaded their old Studebaker with the kids and a few belongings and drove off, without so much as a note. He never saw or heard from her again. Some people claim she went to Winnipeg, while others say they received postcards from as far away as Calgary. But who knows? People move all the time. Some of us, though, like Chickadee, live their whole lives where they were born. So he didn't go looking for Geraldine. If she wanted him, she knew where to find him.

At the time of this story, I worked with him on the sorting floor in the paper mill. We used pickaroons to position eight-foot logs into the right chute. By then, everyone called him Grandpa Chickadee.

He didn't have much to say even when he was drunk, which wasn't that often. When he did drink, it was always at the Lake of the Woods Hotel because he was fond of a certain barmaid who worked there. When he was drunk, he'd sit in the corner yelling, *Fuck'er Livingston Fuck'er*, until a bouncer would throw him out. No one ever discovered who Livingston was.

There wasn't a harder worker in the mill than Chickadee. During a shift, I never saw him stop for more than a minute and only to go take a leak. Most men didn't like to work alongside him because he always made them look bad.

He didn't care what people said about him. Nor did he ever badmouth anyone besides Livingston.

His house was at the top of Barsky hill and not far from the mill. He used to walk to work in the mornings even when it was thirty below. He never wore mitts or a hat, just shoved his hands into his pockets as he walked, only taking them out now and then to rub his ears, which by the middle of winter had darkened from frostbite.

The few times I gave him a ride home after our shift, he didn't say much more than *yes* or *no* to any questions I posed. That suited me just fine.

Most weekends in the fall he went hunting and left town on Friday afternoon, right after work, and never returned until Sunday at midnight. This particular weekend in early November, the sun still had some warmth to it. It had snowed at least a half-dozen times, but that Friday was extra warm for November.

All Chickadee took with him was his 303 rifle and a small pack filled with an extra pair of socks and underwear. He wasn't going for more than a couple days. What else could he need? He always traveled light when hunting. This time, though, he would have been wise to pack a sleeping bag, but he always lit a good fire and that kept him warm at night.

Every hunting trip, he stopped at Redden's Store for last minute supplies before going the rest of the way to East Hawk Lake. That's what he did that Friday in November. Lorne Redden remembers selling him a couple cans of beans, but nothing else. That was enough food to last him the weekend. Afterward, Chickadee hitchhiked the remaining nearly twenty miles to East Hawk Lake. He kept an old canoe hidden on the shore of the lake. So that Friday he paddled his canoe to the south beach and built a fire for the night.

On Saturday morning, he woke to see a large buck two hundred yards from him drinking from the lake. It vanished before he could release the safety on his rifle. It didn't take him long to find the deer's tracks and soon he was skirting the edge of a swamp on one side and creek on the other. Normally all but the deepest rivers and lakes are frozen over by this time of year but a warm few days had slowed the freezing, and had even thawed things a bit. The first snowfalls had melted to patchy spots, so he had to track the deer through slush, where most of the tracks disappeared.

Despite the slush, Chickadee must have thought this was no different than other times he'd tracked an animal and that was another mistake because no two hunts are ever alike. Every creature dies differently and is killed differently. The killing of an animal should never be done without reverence for the life being taken.

Those who went hunting with Chickadee, which weren't many, said he was always respectful of the animals he killed. Also he was different in the bush. Not so restless, more purposeful and steady. He still didn't say much, but somehow he became better company and when he looked a person in the eye the skittish shyness had disappeared. He was more himself. He had a grace and composure that surprised those who went with him.

Occasionally around the fire, or as they waited in a good hiding place, he'd be in a more talkative mood. Mostly he talked about how much he missed his kids and Geraldine.

He rarely smoked or drank when he hunted, although he still sipped coffee now and then. Mostly he sat quietly listening and watching, and everyone said he could hear a deer or moose approaching from half-a-mile.

He usually sat with his knees pulled close to his chest with his 303 resting on his right knee just in case. He was particular about leaving the safety on until the deer or moose was within firing range. To do otherwise would be to hunt dangerously. Part of the challenge for him was releasing the safety and firing as quickly a possible. The slightest sound would be enough to give the animal warning. It was a little test he gave himself and the animal. If it got away before he could fire, it deserved to live.

Chickadee didn't catch up with the deer for the rest of the day, and he must have started to realize then that his legs weren't quite as strong as they once had been. When he was younger, he would soon overtake even the fastest deer, because they usually were careless enough to eat along the way. Besides nature made them best for short bursts, so they tire quickly.

That was another mistake he made, following an animal past the point of prudence. Occasionally, a hunter needs to abandon the trail of one quarry and move on to other animals. To continue hot pursuit for a whole day of a healthy animal is not a wise course of action.

It was getting dark by then and he stopped to make a fire. He wasn't particularly careful about the spot he chose, but he'd been doing this for years without any incident. Habits are another luxury a hunter can't afford. Habits make you easy to find. They might even get you killed.

He built a bed for the fire and assembled dead poplar and pine branches and after he had a good fire going, he ate his first can of warm beans, then lay down and within minutes he likely was fast asleep.

The size of his burned out fire suggested he woke during the night and added wood and poked around in the coals until they flared up again.

That must have been when he heard the first howls. Close enough to get his attention, much closer than he expected given the light from his fire.

More howls followed and each one closer. He checked his rifle and turned the safety off. He added more wood to the fire and poked at it, making sure the wolves could see it from far away. He would have felt safe as long as he had the fire because wolves might approach close enough to sniff, but would certainly move on. Still he would have kept his rifle ready.

The howls must have became very close together and seemed to be gathering inward from several directions. They would be circling him. The leader would hold back, orchestrating every move, his alpha-wolf howls coaxing the others into position.

As the wolves circled Chickadee, he must have prepared as best he could. He also knew that wolves were not like dogs. You couldn't just shoot a couple and the rest would hightail it. The more wolves you kill the more determined their attack.

By the time they stopped howling, he would have heard them cracking through bush. Snapping branches and twigs. Confident enough they didn't try to be quiet.

The mere sight of a wolf pack can cause a deer's heart to explode, the animal dead before the first fangs reach its throat. But Chickadee wasn't a deer. His heart would have hardly sped up. Sure he would have had his thoughts. Doubting thoughts. But he'd been in worse situations than this in his life. During the war, he'd scouted behind enemy lines and had hidden for a week just steps from a German company. Still a pack of wolves will make even the fiercest hunter quake. Being outnumbered does that. Ten to one. Twelve to one. What does it matter? Same damn odds either way.

Wolves always press from behind first. Then when you turn around they push from your flank. They'll advance slowly initially, but as they get closer, they'll bare their teeth waiting for the right moment to attack. Even if an animal like a deer or moose tries to escape, one of them will run it down.

By now the wolves would have been close enough their eyes caught the fire. He would have heard their whines and the *huff, huff*, of their breathing. He could have shot by then and many hunters would have, but he waited until they were close enough that he could pick them off quicker.

The key is killing the right wolf first. Kill the wrong one and you're dead. Kill the right one and you'll get them all one after another. It's not the leader you go after. He'll be in the back watching, because it's vital he survive. Not the weakest one either. No, you have to find the second in command, the beta-wolf, the enforcer and one most likely to replace the leader. He won't be the keenest, or the first to lunge, that will be the weaklings. But he'll be not far behind, showing he can lead if necessary.

When he finally shot in rapid succession, most of them must have died before they could attack although several he may have shot in mid air. That would have provided the most exciting challenge to a marksman like Chickadee.

In no time, he'd killed ten wolves, leaving only two or three. Maybe he shot two of them as they stopped to sniff at a dying companion.

The last wolf must have headed into the bush before he could get off a clear shot.

He wasn't about to follow any animal in the dark. He wasn't a fool. Besides until daylight he'd be busy with their hides.

That's all we know about his final hours. He spent them skinning the wolves he'd shot. Those that examined the hides said he did one hell of a job. Skinned their hides so clean you could hang them on the wall with little additional preparation.

He stacked the skins and dragged each of the twelve carcasses to a different clock-position in a circle around him. Then waited for the last wolf to return because he knew he would. The leader owes that to his pack. Wolves mate for life. Those packs are one extended family. Attack one member you attack the family. That must have been why he sat waiting. Chickadee wasn't about to leave an angry, lone wolf loose in the wild. So he waited.

If he'd been smart and gathered up those hides I wouldn't be telling this story now because there would be nothing to tell. He wasn't the first hunter in these parts to have killed a dozen wolves. That story's been told enough times already.

When Chickadee didn't appear for his shift at the mill on Monday, people noticed, but no one sounded an alarm. Men often don't show up to work on Monday, especially after a weekend of drinking. Still Chickadee was not the type to miss work without some warning and certainly never because he was hung over. The foreman didn't call the police. Perhaps he should have. For years, everyone set the blame there. If the wheels had been put into motion sooner, but then Chickadee was not the type of man the system felt any urgency over. Still, if they had, who knows what would have happened.

On Tuesday, when he didn't show up for his afternoon shift, the foreman called his home but got no answer. He asked around the mill, but no one had seen Chickadee since the end of his shift on Friday.

The foreman sent me to poke around Chickadee's house. When I got there, I knocked out of courtesy, but didn't expect an answer. When I got none, I went inside. No one locked their doors then. Hell few of us had anything worth stealing and few people stole. Especially off people like Chickadee. Thieves were more interested in the big houses on the lake, those belonging to Americans or Winnipers. People who had plenty of money and wouldn't miss some.

The wood stove in his kitchen was dead cold and hadn't been lit in a couple of days. The house was neat and clean, not a bit of clutter in any room. Nothing was out of place. Not at all what I expected. His bed was made so perfectly he could have been in the army. There wasn't much in his bedroom except old pictures of his kids and Geraldine and a wedding picture that hadn't been dusted in years although the rest of the room was spotless.

That was the first time I'd ever been in Chickadee's house. All the times I'd dropped him off after work or drinks, he never once invited me in. I took that to mean that he was ashamed of his place. I figured it had to be in a shambles. But that day I realized he'd just been shy or had lived alone so long he didn't know how to cope with visitors.

I returned to his kitchen and checked the sink for dishes from breakfast or the previous night, but the sink was empty. I opened a few cupboards and each was meticulously arranged, cups on one shelf, glasses on another.

He hadn't been home for a few days. No one leaves a house this neat unless they expect to be away for a while. I called the foreman from Chickadee's house and he told me to get my ass back to work or he'd dock me for an hour's pay even though he was the one that had sent me. I didn't wait for him to call the police though. I called them from there. Told them what I knew and then headed back to work. When I got there, the foreman looked like he was going to chew me out. He even came out of his office and looked my way before he pointed to the sorting floor, which had slowed to a standstill with two men out.

The police arrived about three hours later. A young, pimply fellow, Hutchins was his name. He came from Port Arthur or Sudbury. Some place south like that. He spent a long time in the foreman's office and then came out and talked to us. He had a clipboard and a long list of questions with ticks beside them or a few bits of scribbling. His handwriting was so bad I couldn't make out anything he wrote down. He looked more like a safety inspector.

He asked me questions like:

Did Chickadee have family out of town?

Don't know.

When was the last time I saw him?

On Friday at work.

Did he have a girlfriend?

Not that I know of.

Did he like to drink?

Yes.

Was he drinking this weekend?

Not that I know of.

He asked everyone the same questions. I guess he wanted to be thorough and needed to have the answers corroborated before he wrote them down. Police procedure.

By quitting time, it was on the radio. Chickadee Brant disappeared while hunting. Search parties were formed.

I had to work the next day and the day after. The foreman didn't give anybody time off to search. If they wanted to search, they had to do it on their own time.

That's the government's job. Let the police take care of it. We can't stop the whole plant so you guys can have a holiday tramping through the bush. Hell, half of you'll take the day off and bugger off hunting somewhere and won't bother to search.

He had a pretty low opinion of people.

It wasn't until Saturday, my day off, that I got a chance to join the search. Your mother had her hands full with you guys, but I had to do it.

By then, someone had found his canoe and the authorities had a good idea of where to search. It was still like finding a needle in a haystack, but at least it was a smaller stack by then. I left early in the morning to get a jump on the day. Occasionally a person gets lucky. As I searched, I was certain that Chickadee was dead and I was looking for a body. No one as good as Chickadee gets lost. So he had to be dead. Tourists maybe or kids they get lost that's the end of them first off. But Chickadee he would have made out okay. If he were still alive, he'd have made sure we'd seen him by now, or he'd found his own way to the highway. Hell he could find his way out of any bush between Vermillian Bay and West Hawk Lake. So by now either he had an accident and was holed up somewhere, maybe with a broken leg, or worse was face down dead. It was just a matter of locating where.

There were a lot of black flies and mosquitoes that day. It's very swampy to the south of East Hawk Lake. In no time, my boots were soaked and my neck and arms were being eaten alive. It seemed the black flies and mosquitoes would take turns having their fill. The black flies especially got to me. Dozens of them covered my arms and no matter how much I swatted or scared them off, a minute later they were back.

I wasn't there when they found his campsite. But I wasn't far away and heard the shouts.

Over here! Over here!

That's when we saw the pelts, rifle and pack. An even dozen pelts neatly stacked on top of each other and perfectly encircled by a dozen picked-over carcasses, each with a small cloud of hovering flies.

Several of us eyed the pelts because they could easily fetch a couple hundred dollars. Knowing Chickadee though he would-n't have sold them or taken the bounty. He would have used some in his house and given the rest away. Money burned a hole in his pocket.

His pack and rifle were near the stacked pelts. The rifle lay on a rock as though aimed. What kind of hunter leaves his gun behind? Either scared or stupid, but Chickadee was neither of those.

It looked as if he'd just stood up and walked away for reasons beyond anyone's comprehension. They never found his body. Not then nor anytime since, although plenty of bodies have shown up over the years, but not Chickadee's. Some in the search party followed the tracks of the lone wolf. It wandered back and forth for a good mile but ended at East Hawk Lake. Wolves, like dogs, can swim, but are usually shy of the water, not liking to be out in the open like that. But that wolf must have slipped in and swam away. If it reached the other side, no fresh tracks were found. But then, it's easy to miss things like that in the bush. Even for the best tracker.

Others followed Chickadee's tracks but they soon petered out and disappeared altogether in the middle of the bush. Not at some destination like the lake as the wolf's did.

Tracks don't tell us much. The coming and going of animals, that's about it. Not much more. Certainly those schooled on such things can and did give a fuller more accurate accounting, of what must have happened that day. But once the tracks ran out there was nothing more to follow. They were able to decipher in detail the comings and goings of various other animals, but nothing more about Chickadee.

We searched the immediate area where his tracks petered out without finding any more tracks or signs of him. I was sure he wouldn't have gone far. I mean how far does a man go without his rifle and food? The bush had swallowed him up and it wasn't about to give him up. I'd never seen the likes of that. I mean a good man like Chickadee doesn't vanish without a logical reason. And there wasn't any.

A few of us searched for months when the official search was called off after a week. That's how much Chickadee's life was worth. A week of taxpayers' money. At least that's better than some places where a person's life isn't worth a dime.

That's when the sightings started. Those reported in the bars were discounted but the sober ones were harder to deny. Most of the rumours came from the mouths of good, reliable men. Not storytellers. Some reported nothing more than a sense of being watched. But others were more specific of seeing a figure moving between trees. But in that dense bush it's hard to tell if what they saw was a man or merely the shadows playing tricks. Sometimes people see what they want to see.

I wasn't one to believe such stories at first. Nor did I have any sightings of my own. But I've been in the world long enough not to rule out anything.

Finally we stopped searching altogether. All of us going back to our daily lives.

The sorting floor wasn't the same without Chickadee. Eventually I was moved to the finishing floor. Worked on a forklift moving the rolls of paper onto railway cars. I liked the change.

Each year after, a few of us made a point of hunting out on East Hawk Lake, making one more pass over that same territory just in case we came across something. The bush is like that.

It will keep a set of bones hidden for the longest time and then you'll stumble over them in the most obvious place and wonder how you'd missed them all those years. But you just did. In this case though we never did see any sign of the man. No bones. No article of clothing. No shoes. Nothing. It was as though he'd vanished into thin air. Poof, just like that, he was gone.

Even to this day, there are those who believe he's still alive out there, hunting with his bare hands.

My father liked to emphasize that last sentence and no matter how the story changed from time to time he always ended it with that line. I didn't like the thought of a wild man wandering the bush. I had grown used to the threat of wolves and bears out behind our house, but the idea of a wild Chickadee Brant in the bush really frightened me.

Now I can drive to within twenty feet of where Chickadee vanished, as I did once with my father. Today Chickadee could have just walked down the road to the highway. Who knows why the road is there or where it ultimately leads. The backcountry is riddled with roads criss-crossing and joining in a dozen complicated or seemingly meaningless ways.

When we drove out there, my father was dying and he was having a hard time breathing because of his lung cancer. I think he'd given up by then. Just wanted to see some place where his life might have changed if he'd taken the chance and escaped into the wilds like Chickadee. If only he'd been greedy enough to go for it. But even wild animals don't abandon their young.

He showed me the rock where Chickadee's rifle lay and how it was positioned, and then pointed out where the pelts had been stacked. I believed every word, even if by then his memory wasn't the best. We then made the short walk through a tangle of ferns and brush to the spot where Chickadee's tracks stopped. My father and I marveled at how innocuous it was and how unlikely it was that he met his end there.

If Chickadee were alive as my father claimed then that doesn't explain why he killed all those wolves and neatly piled their pelts. Or why he left his rifle behind. Wouldn't he have needed it to survive? My father had an argument for that too. "Perhaps he didn't kill those wolves, but someone else did and left them there. Perhaps Chickadee scared him off. Or worse killed him and buried him somewhere." That was my father getting fanciful. But there is merit in my father's explanation and the more I consider that version the less certain I am about what really happened to Chickadee.

Some people think that the pack leader waited around for Chickadee to fall asleep and then killed him and dragged his body to the lake. But my father said there was no evidence of that.

This is a story my father told on repeated occasions, most often when he was drunk. Sometimes Chickadee had more children; sometimes he had none, nor a wife. Sometimes Chickadee had a dream. Sometimes he stayed awake the whole night. But through it all the number of wolves never changed, nor did the number of bullets, for those were the kind of details my father, a hunter, paid attention to. Sometimes he meant the story as a warning, one of those fatherly tasks he thought so essential and he performed so judiciously, but most often, it was purely the telling of it he relished, his eyes suddenly animated.

My father's stories were my introduction to the wild creatures that gathered in the dense bush circling our house. Anything was and could be lurking just a few steps away.

My father and Doug Hughes duck hunting behind the Smith farm likely in 1940

Trespass

And forgive us our trespasses,
as we forgive them that trespass against us.
And lead us not into temptation.
But deliver us from evil. Amen.

Lord's Prayer,
Book of Common Prayer (1559)

EVERYONE AT Longbow Lake, except my father, put up *No Trespassing* signs. Most were worried about stray bullets more than vandals. But it seemed to me my father wasn't afraid of anything. Hunters would park along the highway and take the field behind our house. Some were such regulars they waved as they passed. A few took my father with them, though most didn't. We'd hear the occasional shot, but not many, for in truth there were few deer or moose left.

A number of times I saw dead animals being hauled out by happy hunters. The first time was when I was ten and three men carted the carcass of a deer across the field. Judging by the lack of visible effort, the deer couldn't have weighed much and from a distance looked like a large dog. They put the deer down near where my father parked his car. One of the men, fatter than my father, approached the front of the house where my father and I were sitting.

Hello Mickey, he said. Mickey was my father's nickname. *Want us to give you a hindquarter?*

No, that's okay.

The man shook my father's hand and then joined the other two and all three waved before picking up the deer and walking down our road to the highway. My father never accepted any offers of meat from hunters. To him it would have been payment and he didn't want payment. I'm not sure what he wanted except perhaps to be left alone. Also he'd grown up at a time when there were few *No Trespassing* signs, most of the land still belonging to the crown.

I remember the first time I saw a *No Trespassing* sign and asked my father what it meant. He told me the definition of trespassing and offered his opinion of what the sign really meant.

Only a fool puts up a sign like that. Or some grouch who doesn't want to be neighbourly. Someone who thinks the land belongs to him. When I was a boy we shot up signs like that.

No one shot up the signs around Longbow Lake that I know of. I grew up in a respectful time, if a less neighbourly time.

Just because the land can be fenced off, pegged off, doesn't mean a thing. Remember that. This land freezes, dries up, burns, and starts all over again. That's all land ever does. Land is what we walk on and too many people think they own it, but all they own are their bodies and the shoes on their feet.

When I heard the Lords Prayer in church and that line, *Forgive us our trespasses as we forgive those who trespass against us.* I thought of my father and what he'd said and could have wondered if he'd learned what he knew from the Bible, but I knew better because he'd never set foot in church not even to get married. To him they were buildings that were a waste of good wood, stone and glass. The Bible was not a book he opened.

Hunters kept coming for years after I left home for the city. If I'd stayed and bought my own land I would have put up a *No Trespassing* sign, despite what my father said. Life is full of contradictions. That's one of its more pleasant certainties. I can't even really say why I'd put up the sign. Perhaps like the Lord's Prayer says I expect trespasses whereas my father didn't. He spent the last days of his life in an apartment in Winnipeg. In cities we don't put up *No Trespassing* signs. Every yard already adequately fenced. He rarely left his apartment. There wasn't much in the city he was interested in seeing.

I pass a few *No Trespassing* signs on the road to our place on Salt Spring Island. I get a certain comfort when I see them because they remind me of Longbow Lake. Strange how memory works, most of the time it seems to be this unmanageable glob of things that no matter how hard I try I'll never again make sense of, and at other times it's so clear and easily accessible all I need is a cue like a line in a prayer to bring back hundreds of images, even if they bombard me in no particular order, and certainly not unraveling in the order I put them there.

I think of my father as a boy shooting up *No Trespassing* signs and wonder how many shots he leveled at each sign. One, two, a dozen? Does that really matter? What does matter, what truly does matter is the fact that he shot up the signs and knew forgiveness.

Working in the Mill

MY FATHER lost his job in the paper mill in 1959 after thirteen years. His shift foreman then, Mr. Peters, called him into his office after lunch. He was a big man who moved very slowly both in his mind and body. My father knew what he was going to tell him and yet Mr. Peters had to take his time getting to the point, first asking my father about his family and if he'd done any good hunting lately. Mr. Peters liked to talk about hunting but as far as my father could tell, he hadn't hunted a day in his life.

The reason he had to fire my father, he said, was because my father had been missing too much work lately. My father had a good excuse because my mother was in the mental hospital in Port Arthur and Dad was left looking after us three kids, none of us older than eight. But Mr. Peters said that the wood didn't wait for anyone one and an excuse was still an excuse.

Didn't my father have a family member who could help him out with the kids?

No.

Couldn't he afford to hire someone?

Not on what the mill pays me.

Mr. Peters said the mill wasn't in the social assistance business and had no choice but to let my father go. He smiled and shook my father's hand before my father left his office.

No hard feelings, he said before shutting the door behind my father. I could only imagine that Peters smiled after my father left his office as if he'd just done him a favour. It was a spring day and the sunlight was so bright my father shielded his eyes as sweat formed on his brow. He went back to his locker, gathered up his lunch pail—his lunch untouched—and walked to his truck.

He told me years later, he sat in the truck for over an hour listening to the distinctive and varied noises of the mill. He could isolate certain familiar sounds. The high-pitched whine of the electric forklift carrying the tightly wound rolls away from the finishing floor. The metallic scrape and grind of the wood chipper. He said he'd never been so close to tears in his life. He'd loved his job, rough and demanding as it was, it was what he woke for, what he drove to each morning. It fit him as comfortably as the plaid work shirts he wore every winter until he died.

For the rest of his life, he tried to get back to the time before that moment. His life was never the same, never as good after he was fired. He had a whole lot of feelings that day, some bad, some good. What he remembered most though was the anger, how it fused to everything. He saw men drive up and get out of their trucks their hands heavy with their lunch pails and he wanted to punch them in the face because they still had a job, still were welcome. My father never hit anyone in his life that I know of, he wasn't a fighter, but that day was the closest he ever came to being one. As he drove away from the mill for the last time he passed Mr. Peters brand new 1959 Chev Impala and he had to suppress the urge to bump it hard with the solid steel bumper of his 1951 Ford half-ton. Instead, he spit out the window and lit a cigarette waving the smoke away from his eyes as he drove.

My father had a simple philosophy that satisfied him clear to the grave. All work is good. Working in the mill is good. Working for the Department of Highways is good. Work that involved manual labour is best. It didn't tax the brain too much. It occupied him and gave a structure to his day, and to life, he was thankful for and preferred.

After he was fired, he was unemployed for a year and our family lived on nineteen dollars a week Unemployment Insurance. That was a hard year for him. He drank more and stayed up watching TV until the one station we got went off the air at midnight. Mostly he sat in his chair and listened. He'd roll a dozen Old Chum cigarettes and place them on the kitchen table counting them down as he smoked. When he only had five left, he'd roll another dozen. Three dozen a day he smoked.

Whenever he had to drive by the mill for one reason or another, he always slowed to a crawl, looking at the men coming and going, most of whom he knew. Sometimes he'd even park for a time out front and talk to a few of them. He asked how the work was. Did they need anyone? Every time he was told no.

Eventually he'd put the truck in gear and drive off. In a more just world he'd still be working there.

The wildest I ever saw my father get was that year of unemployment. He occasionally even went on a weeklong bender. Then he'd be drunk when I left for school in the morning and drunk when I got home.

Mostly he sat with a beer in one hand and a cigarette in the other not saying much. When he did talk, it was usually in circles always coming around to the mill and being fired, a subject he never tired of.

Once he screamed so loud in the middle of the night he woke my brother and me. We bounded out of bed thinking there was a fire and found him sitting up in bed, his eyes wild and unfocused. He flailed around until we each grabbed an arm to settle him. He woke then and looked at my brother and me with the most confused stare. I didn't know what to say.

You better get to bed. You've got school in the morning, he said after realizing where he was. Then he lay down and went immediately back to sleep.

The next morning, I dreaded getting up for fear my father would have already started a new day of drinking. But he was at the table sipping coffee and had prepared breakfast for us.

He stayed sober for months after that and stopped complaining about the mill. In fact, he rarely brought it up in conversation, which was a great relief to my brother and me. Within weeks, he started work at the Department of Highways where he worked until he retired.

For years, my brother was convinced that it was the two of us grabbing our father's arms that broke the spell he'd been under. But it's more likely that his new job gave him a reason to get out of bed in the morning.

My father flanked by Royal Smith (to his left) and Alice Smith (to his right) in the field behind the Smith house sometime between 1940 and 1942

Shooting Horses

MY FATHER entered the work force early. By twelve, he was already out of school and working fulltime on the Smith farm where he was raised. The Smiths were distant relatives that took my father in when his mother got pregnant too young as people said then, meaning she was an unwed mother. He never knew his mother nor did he realize he'd grown up with family. He'd been told the Smiths were strangers who'd taken him in when his mother became sick and died. That was how shame worked in the 1920s.

The Smith farm was nearly eighteen kilometers east of Kenora by a winding dirt road that eventually became the Transcanada Highway. Kenora isn't farm country but the Smith farm was a rugged exception. The farm consisted of two small fields cut out of the dense bush. The field behind the house was a mere five acres that sloped up at a fifteen-degree angle toward a wall of granite. To the west, the second field was used for pasture because nothing more than patches of rough grass managed to sprout in hard clay, barely a foot thick over bedrock.

Farming was difficult if not impossible. First countless trees had to be cleared and then topsoil hauled in to form a proper nutrient bed over the clay and rock.

It was my father's job to plow furrows and as he did, he turned up more rock than soil.

In spring, the farm would be deluged with water. Streams would appear suddenly from the hills behind the farm as snow melted. As many as twenty or thirty streams soon flooded the field. The water in the streams was always icy cold and eventually fed into the small slough west of the house. Occasionally the pond filled so rapidly that the water spread toward the house. Then Royal Smith blasted relief channels to divert the water.

After the run off, the streams eventually dried up leaving behind large ruptures in the field. My father spent days filling them in with fresh soil he carted out in a wheelbarrow. When that work was finished, he tilled and planted potatoes, tomatoes, lettuce, green beans, cabbage, turnips and onions.

In the dry springs when there wasn't much run off, forest fires threatened from the north. Often my father and Royal were called out to help fight the fires. Once my father was trapped near Breakneck Lake fighting a fire and spent the night in the lake as fire raged on the south shore. He came home blackened from head to toe from smoke and ash. Alice Smith spent a good hour washing it from his hair, face, and hands.

My father liked to be up in the mornings before anyone else. That allowed him time before breakfast to lead the horses one at a time from the barn to the safety of the corral. My father loved the horses and would spend as much time with them as he could. After supper, he'd bring them out bits of apples and other scraps he gathered from Alice's kitchen.

When the horses got too old, Royal walked them into the woods, where he dug a deep hole and then guided the horse down into the hole and shot it. Some horses needed more coaxing than others but each eventually gave in, trusting him to the very end. He only took my father with him once and that was when he had to retire his favourite black mare, *Smokie*. She'd been a difficult horse to break. Royal found her wandering in his field one morning and when no one claimed her, he kept her. It took him a week to get her to take a saddle. Each time she managed to throw rider and saddle off. Once she was broken, though, she was the gentlest animal in the herd.

When the time came to shoot her, Royal couldn't do it and handed the rifle to my father. Three times, he raised it and couldn't shoot. Not with her looking at him. Each time the rifle trembled in his hands and he couldn't get a proper aim. Finally, Royal blindfolded the horse. Then my father approached to within a few feet of her, where he was sure not to miss. He could hear her forced breathing, because she was old with little time left in her. She stood perfectly still as if she knew.

When my father fired, she dropped slowly. First, her hind legs gave one after the other. She stayed like that for a few seconds, and then her front legs gave out and down she went. The two of them then shoved dirt over her, beginning with her hindquarters and working toward her head. A few times her body shuddered as a shovelful struck her.

The spot Royal picked to bury her was a good mile behind

the farm. My father could never find his way back there. But Royal went many times.

That was my father's introduction to killing. It would be years before he'd go hunting. But by then, he was used to killing.

Royal had three huge brown Clydesdale horses with four white feet. They were the best workhorses available at the time. My father liked the workhorses better than the riding horses. He liked to hitch one to a wagon and make the half-day trip into Kenora for supplies. When Royal finally got a truck, he decided to kill the horses. But my father convinced him to let my father keep two. The rest were taken out into the bush and shot.

My father continued to take the wagon with one of the Clydesdales. They were gentle but brave horses that were not easily scared by the sounds of an approaching car. My father sat proudly on the seat while the horse made its slow progress. He could have driven into town but he preferred the pace of horses.

My father beside a large boulder on the Smith farm in the late 1930s

Panda Café

THE CAFÉS in town had names like *The Ho Ho Café, The Bambo Gardens, The Cecil Café, and The Panda Café.* They served hot beef sandwiches, French fries, Denver sandwiches, and milkshakes. Those were special meals to me. On paydays, my father took us for dinner at the *Panda Café* and I always had a hot beef sandwich. The street outside was busy with the racing noise of cars and motorcycles. In summer, tourists filled the streets with American accents. Often they came off boats in the harbour, walked the streets for a while shopping for authentic souveniers made in Japan. Pens or pencils with Mounties on them or maple leafs. T-shirts that said *Kenora*, or *Lake of the Woods.*

My father usually ordered breaded pickerel with potatoes and peas. My mother had a Denver sandwich, as did my brother. My sister ordered a clubhouse. I liked vanilla milkshakes, my brother chocolate, and my sister strawberry. My dad drank coffee and my mother had a strawberry milkshake. We didn't talk much as we ate. I would look at the other families eating the café. Usually, they were more talkative and I thought happier. But looking back now I know there was much happiness at our table too. It just manifested itself quietly, without words.

After we ate we all returned to the 1951 Pontiac except for my father who went into the Lake of the Woods Hotel for a couple beers while we waited. Occasionally, my brother and I went to the Shop Easy grocery store to shoplift. Returning to the car with our pockets full, we giggled as we showed our mother what we'd stolen. She smiled and said they looked good and never asked where we got the money to pay for the stuff. If she minded us shoplifting, she never said. Mostly I stole pens, flashlight batteries, and Oh Henry bars. My brother stole Coffee Crisp bars, screwdrivers, and lighters.

Most people in town considered my brother and me wild, especially my brother, who was drinking in the hotels by the time he was fifteen. I think back to then and I know we were not wild at all. A little hard to manage perhaps but then my parents never tried to manage us. They didn't believe in that. They thought we were just fine the way we were.

By the time, my father returned to the car, he always smelled of beer and cigarettes. He'd kiss my mother's forehead and shout into the back seat, *What you hooligans been up to?* and flash a smile, the proudest father alive.

The Pontiac had a column gearshift, and it was not the easiest car to get into first gear. Sometimes my father would grind gears for a good minute before the transmission properly engaged. People passing would give our car an annoying glance and a wide berth as if the Pontiac was a ticking bomb. My brother would roll down the window and yell at them or poke my sister who sat between us in the wide back seat. He was forever tormenting her. And I guess I was too.

The muffler was missing by then, and as my father pulled from the curb, the car would backfire, and as he revved it higher, it sounded like a small airplane about to take off, or one of the pulp trucks that roared through town headed for the paper mill. The tires were usually so bald there would be no tread left, and in numerous places, the metal bead showed through. I always worried that we'd get a flat tire on the way home or going up our two-hundred-foot, rough-graveled driveway. But we never did. I don't remember my father ever having a flat. With some matters, he was blessed. In most others, he wasn't.

At the corner, my father would stop right in front of the *Panda Café* and with the engine rumbling I would always wish we were still inside because I loved it there with the smells of French fries and gravy filling the air. It seemed like the best place on earth.

When the way was clear, my father turned right gunning the Pontiac. It had such a gutless engine that it chugged through the turn threatening to stall any second. The car didn't have any power until it was properly warmed up, and only on the highway going sixty. Then, it had plenty of torque and had no trouble passing. But in town it lurched and moaned, complaining about everything asked of it.

I dreaded the hill going out of town most because the engine often died on it and my father would have to back all the way down and take a second run at it. Fortunately, my father had gotten into the habit of taking the long way around, past Central School. Then there weren't any big hills until we hit the open highway and the car had momentum.

Even going the long way, the engine backfired every time my

father took his foot off the gas to shift gears. The backfiring never bothered my father who just laughed at anyone who pointed it out as if it were perfectly natural for cars to backfire.

Usually he had a cigarette going and he smiled and even waved at a few people who turned to look at the passing noise. Those on the sidewalks flinched when the engine backfired and that got my dad and brother laughing.

My father never cared what anyone thought. But then, perhaps it was the beer that made him feel that way. Still to me, he was the wildest person in the world and that's when I was proudest of him. My brother was nearly as wild, and in a few years, he'd look just like my father, with a cigarette in his mouth and gripping a bottle of beer in his hand. Next to them, my mother and I were tame, timid creatures, somehow dropped off at the wrong household. My sister was somewhere in between. Not completely wild, but not tame either.

In summer, when we reached the open highway, we'd roll down all the windows and let the breeze blow through the car, our hair going every which way. By the time we got home, we looked a mess. My brother and I were the worse because our hair was long and mangy. My sister and mother usually had the neat sensibility to put theirs in ponytails.

The house always looked so run down after dinner at the *Panda Café*. Every room had so much clutter there wasn't much space left for us.

My father would go to the fridge for a beer and sit down in front of the TV. Sometimes he'd fiddle with the rabbit ears or the horizontal hold until CBC Winnipeg came in better. It was the only channel we got that far from town and even then the picture was so bad we often had trouble making out the action, although the words were always clear. The rest of us soon joined him. That's where most evenings ended. Both the good ones and the bad ones. Our gaze narrowing to that small flicker in the middle of the room.

After dinner at the *Panda Café*, I sometimes stayed in my own room and dreamed about a better future, but on the nights when my favourite shows were on: *The Twilight Zone*, *The Alfred Hitchcock Hour*, or *The Perry Como Show* the sound of Alfred Hitchcock's, Perry Como's, or Rod Serling's voice soon drew me to the front of the TV too.

Bear Country

MY FATHER called our first house at Longbow Lake the *old place* although it wasn't all that old when it burned down. There were many bears out by the old place, but they didn't bother us much. At night, I could hear them going through the garbage. In the morning, my father would straighten up their mess. My mother liked it better when we lived in town where the noises at night were familiar and safe. But out at Longbow Lake on any given night bear or wolves passed by our front door.

Royal Smith sold my father this one-hundred-and-five acre tract of land, just up the road from the Royal's farm, for a hundred dollars. Part of the title agreement was that my father had to clear and cultivate seventeen acres in order to get the deed. Each year he cut a few more trees but never managed to reach that necessary number of seventeen acres under cultivation. Because of that, when our house burned down in 1964, the government took the land back. I'd learned in school that the government was a benevolent force that looked after us when we were sick or hungry. But to my father the government consisted of miserable sons-of-bitches who replaced his name on his deed with someone else's. He fought to no avail for years to get title back, even if beyond the field, the other eighty or so acres consisted of uninhabitable rock, swamp and occasional slough.

After our house burned down, we moved to the old Bellamy place near the junction of Highway 17 and 71. That's when my father started to shoot the bears that came around. The house wasn't sturdy and safe like the one he built. This one was falling in on itself and the floors had all heaved from the cold.

My father had built his house with high windows so that they were bear proof, but the Bellamy place had windows so low to the ground any bear no matter how small could poke its nose on the glass, and many did. The bears came in larger numbers drawn by decades of sewage that had been dumped just outside the back door.

My father didn't like killing bears mainly because he didn't eat bear meat, and he didn't kill what he didn't eat. But they became such a nuisance at the Bellamy place he had to kill a few as a deterrent.

One morning my father stood at the corner of the house peeing, as he did most mornings, and when he looked up a great black bear had reared up on its hind legs less than a dozen feet away from him. Most men would have run for cover spraying their boots as they ran, but my father calmly finished peeing and then turned around and walked inside. He got the 30-30 from under his bed and put two bullets in it, just in case, and went to find the bear. I sat in my room with my fingers in my ears because I hated the sound of loud noises especially guns. My brother followed my father out and stood behind him. The bear hadn't moved. It was either bold or dumb, or both at once.

Even as my father carefully aimed his rifle, the bear didn't budge. According to my brother, who relayed this all later, the bear and my father looked at each other for the longest time having some kind of silent exchange. Then just as my father had his aim properly set the bear got up on its hind feet again and pawed the air and moaned an almost human moan of protest that my father silenced halfway through with a shot. The bear dropped straight down and lay on its side with its legs making running motions.

He'll be dead in a second, my father said to my brother and then lit a cigarette and puffed away.

A couple of times the bear raised its head as if to look around but didn't have the strength to hold it up for long. It moaned one last time, a long, mournful sound I'm sure could be heard clear to the lake.

After my father finished his cigarette, he poked the bear with the barrel of the 30-30 and the bear opened one eye but that was all it had left. Yellowish foam came out of its mouth and its heavy tongue was pushed between its teeth, as it struggled for another breath, which did not come.

My brother and my father dragged it by its hind feet to the truck.

Can't leave it around here, my father said.

I came out to watch him and my brother hoist it into the back of the truck. I remember how pink its tongue was, how yellow its teeth. My brother punched it square in the gut when the bear was finally lying in the bed of the truck. I was appalled by that, fully expecting the bear to protest the indignity with one final swipe of its paws. But dead animals don't fight back. My brother punched it again and then kicked it. Laughing each time.

That's enough, my father said and gestured for my brother to get down off the truck, which he did. My father lit another cigarette and stood in the back of the truck looking down at the bear. Perhaps wanting to remember this moment because we didn't have a camera in those days.

My father kneeled down and moved his cigarette to the corner of his mouth so he could breathe easier. Then he raised the bear's head up so he could get a better look at him, mindful not to blow smoke in its dead face. He held the bear's head only briefly and then let it drop.

Silly bugger, was all he said. Then he too got down from the truck and hopped into the driver's seat.

Come on boys. Lets go to the dump.

Reluctantly I got in the middle and gagged on smoke until my father finally butted the cigarette in the ashtray.

The garbage dump was down a narrow gravel road five miles from our house. For such a narrow road, it was well used and a driver had to pay attention or they could run head on into someone especially at the hairpin turns.

When we got to the dump, a dozen or so vehicles were parked there, and several people stood with rifles aimed down into the pit. As we drew nearer, I saw three dead bears lying in the gravel. At one, a large man posed the bear's head close to his and he smiled as a woman snapped pictures. A similar scene was going on at another corpse a few feet away.

Bear hunters, my father sneered, and then added, *come on boys give me a hand*. I waited in the front of the truck looking out the back window as my father and brother dragged the corpse over the tailgate and let it drop on the ground.

Want a picture? One of men in the crowd asked my father.

Nope, he said.

He and my brother dragged the dead bear to the edge of the large pit and with the help of a couple bystanders tossed it into the mass below.

My father wiped his hands on his pants and walked back to the truck, my brother close behind.

He didn't say a word the whole trip home. Nor did he light another cigarette. Just whistled a couple of tunes I didn't recognize that must have come from earlier in his life.

As he drove up our road he said, *Animals remember how you treat them. Remember that. Even a dead animal remembers. Just because they're dead, it doesn't mean they're gone. There's a right way to kill and a wrong way.*

Animals are no different than us. They want to die for a reason. So only pull the trigger when you've got a good reason. I couldn't let that bear think it belonged around here. This is our house. What if it had been your mother or one of you that it had scared? He wouldn't have held back then. I saw that in its eyes. That bear had killed before.

I didn't know if that were true or just a way for my father to feel better about what he'd done that morning. But I'd liked to believe what he said is true especially about only killing for a good reason.

For months after no bears came around. They could smell death of one of their own. But the rains wash that away and eventually the bears came back. The sweet stink of boiled peaches and the tantalizing aroma of cooked meat were too big a draw.

Many years later, after my father's funeral, I drove out to our old place and saw a dead bear on the highway near the dump. Its bloated body lay on its right side with its stiff legs pointing forward. Someone had cut off its paws and it lay there defenceless and gored in death. I couldn't tell if it had been hit by a car or shot coming from the dump.

As I sat in my idling car and looked at the dead bear, I thought *the dead merely get in the way of the living.* Then I remembered that day at the dump years earlier with the crowd so eager to kill bears. None of those self-proclaimed hunters were interested in the bears or their claws, only in the kill, and the ease with which each bear took a bullet, dropping before the shot stopped echoing.

Ghost Lake

GHOST LAKE was a mythical lake that only a few people, including my father, claimed to have seen. When my father was twelve or thirteen, Royal took him to see it. Royal heard about the lake from elders in the First Nations' camp near Royal's farm. Every winter they'd set up tents a few miles from the farm and trade deer and moose meat for milk and eggs. The elders said that every spring when they packed up their tents they headed to the shores of Ghost Lake, where they camped for the summer. They said only good people could see the lake and that a bad person would walk right into it and be halfway across before they realized it was there. Most of them drowned.

According to my father, Ghost Lake was five miles north of Royal's farm and was only about a 1/4 mile across, but so deep it didn't have a bottom. Toss a stone in it and the stone would fall forever. The lake was so plentiful with pickerel and lake trout that fishing was as easy as dipping in a hand. The water was so clear he watched large schools of pickerel dodging each other only inches below the surface.

When my brother and I were teenagers, we spent a summer

in search of Ghost Lake. Nearly every morning, we'd pack a lunch and walk due north as my father instructed. No matter what route we took, in no time we'd reach water. We swam in a dozen different lakes over that summer. But none of them had the mystically clear water of Ghost Lake. These were lakes full of tadpoles and bottomed by leeches. Any fish in those waters was bound to be God-awful ugly bottom feeders. Catfish or suckers

When we'd had enough of swimming, we'd circle the lake in search of berry patches. Wild strawberries and raspberries in early July, blueberries later. We'd eat our fill before returning home with hands dyed red or stained purple.

It was while we were picking blueberries one afternoon in early August that I thought I saw water shimmering between the trees. When I went to investigate, I saw another lake through the spruce boughs, a little more north of where we'd normally stopped. I left the blueberries to my brother and set off to explore on my own.

At the first, I lost sight of the lake, but I climbed a nearby poplar and it came back into view. This time I fixed on its location and continued in that direction. From the tree, it appeared not to be far, but I as I walked, it didn't get any closer, and I wondered if it was a bigger lake than I first thought.

Finally, after I'd been walking for about half an hour, I reached it. The lake was the right size to be Ghost Lake, but its water was filthy brown. I knelt down to test the water and it was icy cold.

Just then, I heard a scream and turned in time to see my brother charging straight at me. He must have been tracking me the whole time. He pushed me into the water, clothes and all. I screamed and grabbed at the bank but couldn't pull myself out. *Asshole*, I shouted at him and called him other names too as he stood smiling down at me. That is when I felt them. Little nudges at first against my leg and then they become more urgent, and when I felt around I realized that hundreds of fish surrounded me.

Help! I yelled at my brother who must have seen the terror in my eyes because he dropped to his knees and quickly pulled me out.

Jesus, what did you do that for? I swatted at him but he was too busy looking in the water to notice.

Look, he said, fascination in his voice.

I joined him at the bank and the water was roiling from the tails of huge silver fish. My brother reached in, pulled one out, and tossed it on the bank. It must have weight five pounds.

The fish lay gasping on the ground. It had an ugly head with large deformed eyes. Maybe the lack of light caused the eyes to mutate. I kicked it further up the bank over earth, which smelled strongly of dead fish. Half decayed or stripped carcasses were scattered everywhere. Bears had feasted here recently. The thought of that made we want to head home, but when I turned back to the lake my brother had stripped and jumped into the water and was trashing around to keep the fish away. His feet struck something on the bottom and he gave out a yell. He struggled for a moment and then hoisted out a rusted bumper. He searched around some more in the water for car parts and ended up throwing another fish up onto the bank before getting out.

My brother wrapped up the larger of the two fish and put in his pack and then we left for home. When my father saw the fish he said it was some strange kind of trout he'd never seen before. We called them Ghost fish because of the way their colours camouflaged them and made them hard to see in the water.

My brother and I were curious about the bumper of the car. *How did that get in there?* My brother asked.

At first, my father didn't believe us and thought we were making it up.

Maybe there was a road there a long time ago, before the war, and it has since grown over. My father finally said. *There used to be all kinds of roads out here before the highway.*

I wondered how many other cars were rusting away on the bottom of that lake. I wondered too if they had something do with the fish being so deformed. My brother and I decided to call it Rusty Lake although years later I learned its proper name was Puma Lake.

My brother and I never did find Ghost Lake and by the end of summer, I started to wonder if Ghost Lake wasn't just another of my father's drunken stories that he kept telling because he wanted them to be true and if he told them often enough they might be.

My father and mother at my aunt's farm in
River Hills Manitoba in August 1957

Wild, Hazel Eyes

MOST OF MY mother's sisters and brothers were wild, but she wasn't, at least, not until she turned thirty-five. That's when she began to lose her mind, and she became the wildest except for Orchid, her youngest sister. Orchid died on the side of the road outside Dryden just months shy of her fortieth birthday. Someone had drugged her and left her there in the cold to die. Her frozen body wasn't found until months later, and by then, the police weren't too interested in solving another unsolved murder.

Like my mother, Orchid had wild, hazel eyes that darkened in bright sunlight. She was very nervous and eventually developed a tick in her left eyelid. Most of her adult life, she rarely sat still for long as though something had scared her as a girl and she never got over it. When she was in a good mood, she talked constantly, leaving little room for others to say much. Other times, she wouldn't say a word for days, staying in bed with the covers pulled over her face and complaining that bears were scratching at her window or weasels were hiding under her bed. She'd make my uncle Frank check four or five times an hour to ensure there was nothing lurking. The slightest squeak or scratch of branch on the window was enough to cause her to scream at the top of her lungs.

She never talked in voices like my mother, but spoke over everyone else and if people stopped listening to what she said, she was happy to keep talking. Whenever we visited them in Dryden, I never knew which version of my aunt would greet us. In those days, I preferred the quiet version because she didn't scare me and hid in her room most of the time, and I didn't need to see her. When she was like that, only my mother would go in and sit with her. For hours, my mother would tell her stories and generally keep her company. Sometimes it would lift Orchid's spirits enough that she'd come out and join us for supper. She'd quietly eat the meal that Frank had prepared, and her eyes shifted between us as if we were total strangers.

Or she'd giggle and say something completely off topic like, *Dad has liver disease.* (Her father was already dead by then, had died of a stroke, and had never had liver disease. He never drank much alcohol).

After supper, she'd sit close to the airtight heater and though the stove was blaring hot she'd say she was freezing even as sweat beaded off her red face. Eventually my mother would coax her back to bed and stay with her until she fell asleep.

By then, Orchid had ten children the youngest was five and the oldest nineteen. Every time we visited them, kids would be running wild, and in summer, the youngest ones had nothing on. They didn't have any house rules. No set bedtime. No curfews.

When the drinking replaced the mood swings, she'd sleep

until three or four in the afternoon and be drunk again by sunset. Her husband, Frank, remained sober long enough to fix a proper dinner. Afterward, he'd sit with my father getting pissed after Orchid went to bed.

Frank was a big man and could drink two beers to every one of my father's. They sat in the living room sharing a case of twenty-four O.V. open at their feet and they'd be chugging beers so quick that in no time half the case would be empty.

By then, my mother was the only sober adult protecting thirteen kids. She told stories in the bedroom away from all the drunken noises. The fourteen of us stayed in that crowded bedroom away from the boisterous parts of the house.

Sometimes Orchid would yell a string of curses from her bed always ending with a stretched out, *Frank, you fucker.*

I'd then hear his firm stomp toward their bedroom where there would be more yells and swearing until he'd stomp back and ask, *more beer Mickey?*

My father would pass out on the couch, before the case of beer was empty. I'd hear Frank opening the final few bottles tossing the caps against living room wall. He'd sing to himself, the words muffled. If Orchid was still awake, she'd yell for him to shut up, but he'd then sing louder. When he drank the last bottle, he'd slide the empty case along the floor and say, *Fuck it,* before trudging noisily off to bed.

The house would be so peaceful then. I'd look around at the room full of sleeping children and only my mother and I would still be awake, wide-eyed and worried.

The following morning my mother would get up even before the youngest, making us breakfast and no matter how much noise we made it wasn't enough to disturb my father, Frank, or Orchid until late afternoon.

My father would wake first stretching out his arms on the couch and looking around as if lost. He'd sit up and be all smiles at first as though he'd slept through all the bad in his life and was waking to the good parts. That mood usually didn't last long. After a few beers, the clouds reappeared and he must have remembered again the things that irritated him.

The last time I saw Orchid alive was after just such a night. Except she was up early with my mother, and when I woke, I found them laughing in the kitchen. My mother's visits usually lifted Orchid's spirits. Perhaps she finally had someone around who took her side.

She was making pancakes, while my mother was putting out plates. There was already a rather large stack of pancakes on the long, melamine folding-table they used to accommodate all their children. Frank had bought the table at an auction.

I'm not sure what my mother and Orchid had been laughing at, but when I appeared in the kitchen the laughing stopped. I wanted to retreat, leaving them to whatever fun they were having, but my mother grabbed my hands and examined them.

You'd better wash, she said. She had to hound my brother and me to wash our hands, because otherwise we seldom did. I went to the kitchen sink and washed my hands. All the dishes from the day before had been washed and put away. The room was spotless.

Why don't you go get some sun? Orchid said, and patted me on the head. When she got close to me, she smelled of roses and dishwater.

Later at breakfast, Orchid and my mother busily served everyone, and for once, the children sat still and attentive their faces clean, and each body fully clothed. My mother and Orchid let my father and Frank sleep through all the breakfast smells and coming and goings. When they did wake up in the late afternoon, they were not served pancakes, but were left to fend for themselves. My mother and Orchid had gone for a long walk.

When they got back, I could see by the red of Orchid's eyes she'd been crying. My last image of Orchid is of her slightly puffy eye as she gave my mother a long hug.

Thanks, she said, and then headed for bed.

Frank, sober and not very talkative, saw us to the car. He gave my mother a short hug, shook my father's hand, and then went back inside to attend to dinner.

Not long after that visit, Orchid left one morning after finishing the dishes. The kids were all in school when she put on her best dress and hitchhiked into Dryden. Neither Frank nor the kids ever saw her again.

For months after there were sightings of her with one group of drunks or another. Stories surfaced too of her sitting on different men's laps and others of her passing out in the back of someone's car. Nothing lasted for her. She never called her kids nor sent a letter. She planned to be gone for good.

Uncle Frank stopped drinking then. Got the kids ready for school in the mornings and went to work in the mill. Became an upstanding citizen.

The sightings of Orchid stopped and even those who had been friends with her had no idea where she had gone. The police searched the usual places at the prompting of my uncle. But for all they knew, she could have run off with any number of men. Gone to Winnipeg or Thunder Bay the usual places people went to disappear. If she showed up, fine, if not, it wasn't their problem. They had plenty of other cases to keep them busy.

A young man walking to town in the spring, found her partly clothed body lying by the side of the road, where it had been all winter, preserved by it having been frozen until spring thaw.

My mother took me to Orchid's funeral and it was a closed casket service because she had decomposed by the time they found her. I was grateful for that because I didn't want to see her. After the services, Frank came over to my mother with the youngest in tow. He embraced my mother and I could tell by the way she stood that it made her uncomfortable. She didn't move though just waited for him to stand back. She bore him no malice despite how she felt he'd worked Orchid to the bone with all those kids, and if he'd been a better father, Orchid wouldn't have left.

My father stood at her side with his arm around her and she leaned toward him. That was the most physical affection I ever saw between them.

A few weeks later my mother had her second nervous breakdown and was sent by train to the mental hospital in Port Arthur. She talked in voices, stern scornful voices that seemed to rise out of her sister's death. Blaming voices as if somehow she should have intervened.

After that, my mother never lost her wild streak. There would be months of unexplained calm interrupted suddenly by bursts of mania. Once she ran off and hid in the bush for a week. Fortunately it was summer and the nights were warm enough she managed okay. When we found her, she'd fashioned a cozy little den in a thicket. The grass was neatly packed where she'd slept and in the corner she'd molded a chair out of rock and moss.

My father had no choice but to call Social Services even though he knew it meant she'd be sent again to the mental hospital in Port Arthur.

Much of the handling of mentally ill patients in the 1950s was cloaked in secrecy, as though to openly acknowledge mental illness was to bring shame on the whole community. So each time she was sent back to Port Arthur, they came for her late in the day. She was given a few minutes to pack and then they whisked her away. None of her family was allowed to accompany her to the train station, although we were never told why. So the last we'd see of her for six months or a year would be when she was forced, usually against her will, into the back of a police car.

On the train to Port Arthur, she'd sit by the window closing her eyes for long periods of time. The woman accompanying her would give her a concerned glance every now and then, before returning to the book that she was reading. My mother refused to say more than the bare minimum to her escort.

At the station in Port Arthur she'd feel renewed panic around so many people and not a friendly face amongst them. She'd be taken in a taxi to the hospital where she'd be stripped and told to put on a hospital gown. Every window had bars on it and no matter how hard they tried to say it was a hospital it was still a prison.

She'd sit on her bed for days and not talk to anyone except herself. Sometimes she'd go to a window and look for Lake Superior and the sight of glimmering water in the distance would remind her of home.

Usually after six months or a year, my father would get a letter from the hospital asking him to come and get her.

She'd leave us wild and uncontrollable, and return docile and compliant after months of shock treatments. She spoke slower then, with vacant pauses between sentences. But at least there was only her own voice alive within her for a while.

There Must Have Been Giants

WHEN I WAS a boy, like most kids I believed in giants. However in the stories my mother told me, her giants lived normal lives with jobs, homes and families. They were responsible and didn't wreck havoc but went about their lives as quietly as possible. Some of them were clumsy and made a lot of noise, but most had grace and poise. They lived tragic lives and died horrible deaths. Some fell over ravines others wiped out whole villages simply by taking a wrong turn on the way home from work. They had to live with that guilt for the rest of their lives.

My mother's giants were either afraid of their size or ashamed of it and dreamed of being smaller. Few thought to use their size to their advantage. Their deep voices shook the ground as they spoke and deafened little boys if they got too close.

Her giants feared humans, much as elephants fear mice. Most lived in cities and towns, and like humans were afraid of the wilds and went there seldom. They did not like to hunt or fish, nor did they feel any great need to commune with nature.

They're all dead now. Extinct. Killed one by one. Not by war, pestilence, or famine. But by failing to breed. They simple came to the end of the line and that was it. First families had two children, then one, and soon enough families had no children at all. The last giant born lived a very long life much of it spent alone with only humans for company. He eventually grew tired of their nonstop talking and bickering, and one day, without saying a word to anyone, the last giant started walking north. When the grass turned to snow, he didn't turn back. When the snow turned to ice, he kept walking. Finally at the very northern tip of the world, he lay down on the ice and closed his eyes and never opened them. According to my mother, his frozen body is still there, waiting for someone to come and haul it some place warm to bury.

Killing Suckers

EACH SPRING suckers returned to the creek across the highway to spawn. My brother and I would get together with the Paquette boys to kill as many suckers as we could. One of us threw the fish onto the bank and the others would club them. We'd fashion spears out of branches and see how accurate we could be, but it didn't take much of an aim to hit something.

The heaving and clubbing worked the best. I didn't care much for this activity and usually sat on the bank refusing to participate. But still I came along to watch and did nothing to stop the slaughter. My brother and I had forgotten our father's warning to only kill animals for a good reason.

The slaughter was hard to watch at times and I hated how the dying fish flapped around. For days after, the bank of the creek would reek so much we could smell the rot from the highway. I'd watch birds circle the gruesome piles.

It still strikes me as strange how we have very definite hierarchies when it comes to animals. Some we allow to sleep in bed with us, others we're happy to club over the head. We never ate any of the suckers. Who eats suckers? Only the very hungry. I can't think of a less desirable fish to eat. They are ugly-faced bottom feeders whose flesh is wormy and bony and tastes spoiled no matter how it's prepared.

We were just boys, a good number of years from manhood. We bounded with energy and needed things to do.

I'm not sure what impact we made on sucker populations or what would have happened to them if humans hadn't seen it fit to slaughter them.

The last time, I went killing suckers was the spring I turned fifteen. Only my brother and I went because the Paquette boys had gone to work cutting wood for their father.

I hadn't really been keen on going, but my brother coaxed me. I refused to take a club with me, and so neither did my brother. I sat high on the bank and watched him toss nearly a dozen suckers onto the bank. We left them to die in the early June heat. The run was lower than previous years, and as we walked along the creek to the highway, I saw a much smaller dark circle of them in the water. I looked back on the ones my brother had left on the shore and already several birds were pecking at them. I realized those birds had grown used to us providing them with an ample spring feed of suckers, saving them the trouble of having to dive in and get them on their own. As we reached the highway, there was a greedy gathering of gulls and crows fighting over the few suckers.

Perhaps other boys came later that day or in the days following to toss them food on the shore, but not likely because there weren't any other kids living out our way.

The dying suckers had such round, pursed mouths as if they sucked futilely on air. Now I know the purpose of such an animal. Their mouths make it easy for them to siphon food off the bottom hence they help keep rivers and lakes cleaner. They might not be beautiful, but they serve a very an important function in the chain of all life.

In any case, I am certain that boys continue to slaughter suckers along the creeks and rivers of northwestern Ontario, although the sucker populations have been greatly depleted. We were no different, killing the greedy human way and thinking it grand.

My father throwing snowballs with Lindy and Yvonne Hatley at Longbow Lake around 1935

Bear Attack

My father was nearly fifteen when he saw what a bear could do to a man. He was riding into town on the Royal's black mare. He was happy that day. At least that is how he told it.

I'VE NEVER BEEN afraid of beers, but that doesn't mean they haven't given me a cause for worry. When I was eight, Alice's sister had a run in with one. She was a few weeks pregnant at the time, and her husband was in town working. The bear tore open the front door of their cabin and then ate its way through the kitchen tossing flour and rice everywhere. When it was full, it went back out the front door.

The whole time the bear was in the house it ignored Alice's sister who hid in the bedroom. She thought about escaping out the bedroom window but she didn't really have anywhere to run, because her nearest neighbour was two miles away.

When the bear left, she worked so hard putting the front door back on and cleaning up that she lay down exhausted. When she woke, the bed was full of blood and she wept. The next day she bought a 303 rifle and kept it in reach at all times. She never did have any children.

That was nothing, though, compared to what I saw a few years later. One day in early June, Royal sent me for some goods he wanted in a hurry. I had to ride fast to escape the black flies. The road into town was more of a horse trail than something cars could properly use, although some did. I knew shortcuts through the bush and took them wherever I could. I shouldn't have been doing that with his best horse, but I did.

I was on one of those shortcuts when Royal's horse practically stepped on the body. Might have too, if I hadn't laid eyes on him just in time and pulled the horse up short. I was crossing just above Hilly Lake. The highway follows on the other side of the lake now. But then you could look in every direction and see nothing but wilderness.

The guy had been dead a day or two by the look and smell of him. The sight of someone dead didn't bother me. I've never been shy of dead animals or people. I'd seen my share of death on the farm. But the smell now that was different. You never get used to the smell of rot. I don't care who you are it's bound to turn your stomach.

As I got close, I saw that an animal, most likely a bear, had clawed large chunks of flesh away from the man's skull. I had no idea how his corpse got left there nor why the bear had attacked. There was nothing to make sense of it. He must have been walking to town. He'd been a bald man although it was hard to tell after the bear was finished with him. He had no identification on him, but that was common then. I searched the vicinity for any signs of bear, but it was likely miles away by then.

I figured the poor guy probably surprised a sow and her cubs because that's the main reason a black bear will attack.

I left the body where I found it and went to the police station as soon as I got to town. They were curious at first, asked me plenty of questions, but took their time going out there after him. They told me to do my errands for Royal first and they'd follow me back.

A dead man's not going anywhere, the duty officer told me. He also said that the man was probably some unlucky prospector too busy looking for gold to have any sense about him.

Two young constables came with me. Most of the way out they rode behind me, telling jokes. When we reached the corpse, the younger of the two dismounted and turned the dead man over while the other watched from his saddle. I didn't stick around because there was only an hour or so of daylight left and besides I didn't want to keep Royal waiting. Before the trail turned, I looked back and they were laughing as they hoisted him onto the spare horse they'd brought. They didn't notice me leave and apparently didn't care. They had a hard time getting him onto the horse although I knew he wasn't that heavy. One balanced him while the other crudely tied him into place.

The older officer slapped the horse and watched it sprint on ahead down the trail. Quickly they were on their horses chasing after it, having as much fun with a dead body as they could.

That was the last I ever saw of them or the dead man. I did read in the newspaper the next week that the police searched for a couple days for that bear. This was before there were helicopters and airplanes for such a thing. Everything was done on foot or horseback. The tracks petered out eventually and the bear had too good a head start for it ever to be caught. The police warned that the bear would be back and that when it returned it was almost certain to be even more aggressive, more dangerous, more likely to kill.

But it never came back. Maybe some hunter killed it before the year was out or the bear went up north to Pickle Crow or somewhere the fishing was good enough to make it stick around. Maybe it lived a good long life up there.

The man wasn't a prospector, but a hunter from Chicago. They found his camp not far from his body. His rifle still lay against his tent. The bear must have surprised him while he was taking a leak. His powerboat was tied to the dock in town. He had a wife and kids in Chicago and she came up with her brother and took the body back in their boat. Seemed such a waste of a life. He thought he was a better hunter than he was. Tourists should never hunt alone.

Hunting buddies of my father in Kenora during the winter of 1941

Flagging on the Highway

MY FATHER sits in the hot sun flagging traffic. He has on a blue t-shirt the kind he always liked to wear. A plain blue t-shirt and his freckled arms are brown from the hot sun. All summer he wears his red hardhat directing traffic around the sign crew. He is in his early sixties and stands bull-legged. In his back pocket he has a pair of pliers and a handkerchief. The pavement is hot under his feet and he has to keep shuffling to cool them. Behind him somewhere, a crew of three young men are lifting a heavy sign into place. He once did that work but he's too old to do it now.

After work he sits down at the kitchen table expecting dinner. My parents don't say much eating quietly through the meal. After supper, he sits on his bed in front of the TV and watches it while having a beer. All the windows are darkened to keep the heat out and to cut the glare off the TV screen. So even though it is hours before the summer sun goes down it appears night-time.

This is how my parents spend the final years before my father's retirement. The routine of their days hasn't changed since I left home. Not much changes, in their lives except on the weekend, when my father drinks to cut down on the boredom of not being at work.

While he flags traffic on the highway, my mother cleans house, then goes for a walk, even takes a swim in the lake. Their lives haven't turned out as they planned. My father thought he'd be a baseball player or a long distance trucker. My mother thought she'd be a rich songwriter or at least marry someone with money.

In the summer, they sit out and listen to the frogs and crickets. My father sips a beer and drags on his cigarette. My mother sits next to him fanning the air with her hand. She does most of the talking. Occasionally they hold hands. When it gets too dark, or chilly, they go in and go to sleep in separate beds. My father stays up late, watching TV until it goes off the air, my mother already sound asleep.

She no longer needs to go to the mental hospital because she now has effective drug treatment.

They are a relatively happy couple.

September

This is one of the last stories I remember my father telling me. At the time of the telling, the weight of worry had shifted from his shoulders to mine.

DID I EVER tell you about how Neil Chambers came to hate September? For years, Neil loved that month most of all because his children would get out from underfoot and head back to school. That put his wife Gladys into a better mood and when Gladys was in a good mood all was right with the world. Sometimes she'd even feel like making love, which might be hard to believe after nine kids.

On the first day of the new school year, Tommy, the oldest, lined the other kids up, usually by age. From his van Neil watched them fidget and chatter as they waited for the bus. During the summer, their noises drove him and Gladys batty, but from his van, they sounded like pure joy.

Children can grow to hate a father for many different reasons. Some of them justified, others founded on little more than his manner. Not that Neil was mean to the kids or anything. But after that September Tommy was the hardest hit because he was old enough to understand the rumours and to pay attention to what other kids said. Tommy was a bright boy good with machinery like his father. He was always fixing bikes or lawn-mowers—small things like that. The other kids looked up to Tommy and if he started to feel differently about their father then they did too. Tommy liked to spend a lot of time by himself. I used to see him sitting on the bank of Longbow Lake fishing.

The other reason Neil loved September was because his work got easier as the camps and resorts began to close. He repaired refrigerators and refrigeration units, big ones like those in hotels and hospitals. He was good at his job, the best in town in fact, and unfortunately, that meant longer hours in the summer. With eleven mouths to feed, he needed all the work he could get, so he never turned down a job, and sometimes he was even called out in the middle of the night. In the heat of the summer, having no refrigeration is extremely bad for business.

But starting in September, he could take a day or two off. Then he and Gladys wandered around the trailer gathering in the quiet. Sometimes they'd make love all afternoon dressing again before the kids got home. Their lovemaking was quiet, but inside it ran a glorious seam of pure pleasure. It was the one time Neil felt his life elevated above the ordinary. It was on those days off that the two of them talked without interruptions, made plans and remembered what brought them together in the first place. The rest of their days were pure chaos.

Gladys was the one who held the family together. Neil wasn't particularly good with people even his own children. I'm sure he loved them. Neil's skills were with fixing refrigerators not people, no matter how hard he might have tried. If someone had a problem with refrigeration, he was the one to call. He had an uncanny ability to diagnose any refrigeration problem. All he had to do was put his hands or head to the unit and he knew. But give him a problem of the heart, like a lovesick teenager, and he was completely lost. That's when Gladys took over.

She tried to keep the children well behaved but there always was one or two at any given time out of control, and by the end of the day, who cares as long as no one gets hurt. Jerry and Donald, the twins, fought most of the time and it was usually Neil who had to pull them apart.

The day September changed for Neil, old man Baxter, who owns Baxter's Store, was one of the first at the dock. What he was doing in town that time of day is anybody's guess because he was usually at his store twelve or fourteen hours a day even in September. There were too many tourists around yet for him to close.

His store is three miles closer to town that Neil's place. He had one or two beat up cabins on Longbow Lake, but tourists were happy to pay a premium just to be on the lake. Those few impatient ones who couldn't wait for the mile or so for the big tourist camp up the highway or those who liked a quaint beat-up place like Baxter's or liked the idea of roughing it in the bush even if the Transcanada Highway went right past them.

Baxter wasn't as sharp now that his daughter and her husband had taken over the business, but he was in the store every day talking to the locals or tourists that stopped by to stock up on this or that. But he was in town that day and saw Neil in a boat approaching the dock. Nothing unusual in that not at least until the boat got close enough for Baxter to see.

That summer Neil had spent working out on Lake of the Woods. He rented a barge in town so he could take his van with him out to the various islands where he was working. He was making good money too. He worked past dark most days finding his way back to Kenora between the islands by reading the lights along the lake. Neil never got lost. I don't even think he thought it was an option.

By September, he was working at Hay Island on the big coolers in a lodge there. The couple that ran it were from the United States though they had Swedish accents. He only understood about half of what they said, but he never let on. The husband was a real bastard. His name was Ben Holm and his surname had been changed from Holmstrom or something. Ben was the suspicious type in the first place and was always checking Neil's work, which was one thing Neil could never abide. People watching him work made him nervous. So, Neil was having a particularly hard time repairing Ben's two coolers. He worked there only every other day fiddling for a few hours then went off to some other job. Sometimes Neil had a short attention span especially if someone was watching him. Half his kids are like that. It would drive anyone crazy.

Neil began to spend more time on Hay Island than anywhere else, and Garth Turner, who lived up the lake from Hay Island and took his boat once a day to town to check his mail, told me he saw the barge early one morning too early for Neil to have gone out in a normal morning of work. Garth figured it had been there all night. Garth was not one to lie or make things up.

Hay Island is a lonely place at the far end of a long bay that most people don't go directly past it on the way into town. On the opposite end of the island from the lodge was a trapper's cabin free to anyone who wished to use it. I've stayed there myself several times.

The island is up the lake far enough to be severed some from the influences of town but not far enough to be completely lost to the influences of humans. It's hard to know what happens to people when they start to lose the grip of their own societies. In the wild, we often become the creatures we'd like to forget even though our societies are shaped in every way by that very thing. It's hard to say most of the time what drives us. Sometimes I think it is nothing more than lunacy as we seek along the shores of a great lake like this, more and more places to build.

Some people think Neil's children drove him to it. I'm not sure that's true, but you be the judge. I'm not sure if it was the same day Garth saw Neil's barge so early in the morning or not but near two that afternoon people saw Neil in the Holm's eighteen foot boat going full throttle, his head bent down against the wind or perhaps he was looking at something in the boat. The wife was all alone that day and I suppose he should have known better, should have backed his way to the barge as quickly as possible but he didn't.

The lake was so rough he nearly capsized once, but kept going.

He'd already taken their boat into town once that day to get parts. His barge was too slow to make the round trip. He'd been seen in town at the warehouse getting copper pipe. Later at the dock, he bought gas, but too much for just the trip back.

While he was in town, the husband came back with the bigger boat. The one he kept in the boathouse most of the time and only took out when he had paying customers. But it had been a slow summer and not many people had been willing to pay for a few days excursion up the lake to the real open waters of the Big Traverse.

He must have returned while Neil was in town and found her. Who knows? None of them seemed to be people drawn to guns or the things guns made you do if you weren't careful. None were hunters especially Neil who spent the hunting season working the way he spent most seasons.

From here on everyone's version of the story is different and the only one not telling is Neil. Any time a crime occurs everyone becomes a suspect. People will question things even if the authorities don't, especially here, where everyone minds everyone else's business.

The story goes that Neil found them in the kitchen. One had fallen back into the open cooler the other on the floor. The husband's face was blown away by the shotgun. Some think Neil killed them both and brought back the woman to make him look innocent. Claiming she was still alive. But you can't save someone by water that far out the lake. Why didn't he phone for a floatplane? Nothing completely added up even if it did enough for the police. Besides Neil was from around here so of course the police would believe his story. Anyway, the authorities like the simplest version best. And murder/suicide is so easy to believe, especially there. What happens out on the lake, happens in its own time and place and is mostly outside our influence.

It's certainly strange to me how he only took her body into

town. Some said she didn't look like someone shot. Just dead. He laid her on the dock and ignored those who came to look. He didn't even recognize old man Baxter bent over the body. Neil got Baxter to back up his car and then Neil loaded her inside. No one else bothered to help, they were all so shocked. Those who were there said he looked pale and babbled the whole time.

Baxter drove them to the emergency door of the hospital and they waited for the police. Some said she'd only been dead a half an hour, others said hours. Later the town was buzzing with rumours. Old man Baxter was a good one for rumours and theories. Crazy theories he must have dreamed up in his store when business was quiet. It was Baxter who said they found Neil's sperm in the woman during autopsy.

Neil never was paid for all his work on them coolers. That is hard on a man with nine kids. The investigation was closed almost overnight. Police don't listen to rumours. If they did, half the people in town would be arrested. The uncertainty remained.

Neil and his family moved away. The road to what once was their trailer is barely visible anymore. I went up there recently, stood at the door to the trailer, and looked inside. Amongst the few pieces of furniture left behind, bushes were growing up through the floor.

There is another version of the story, where Neil surprised Holm in the process of killing his wife, shot him in the face with the shotgun, and tried to rush Mrs. Holm to the hospital. I suspect that is Neil's version although not the one he told the police. That one he told straight. He found them both shot.

The wife was still breathing so he did the best he could to save her.

If she was still alive, what did she tell Neil as he leaned forward in the boat keeping it steady over that bumpy water while he held her hand the whole final stretch into town? Did he feel her slip away with each pound of the boat? Did he even hear what she said above all that noise?

Afterword

SHORTLY BEFORE my father died in 1995, I drove him for the last time from Winnipeg to Kenora and Longbow Lake. By then the Transcanada Highway went directly through the middle of the field behind the Smith farmhouse. There was an interchange where our house had once been. We stopped in to see some of my father's friends, and when he spoke frankly of his lung cancer, his eyes had a sparkle that I hadn't seen in years. He was never one to give into despair despite all the hard turns in his life.

I stopped the car at what had once been the start of our driveway and asked him if he was glad to see all the familiar places again.

No. There are too many memories here, he said.

At the time, I thought that was a peculiar thing to say, especially given that ever since he moved to Winnipeg ten years earlier he had often complained about missing Longbow Lake. Then I still considered memories sacred and needful.

Five years later when I visited the very same place with my partner Pearl, I suddenly knew exactly what he meant.

Everywhere I looked some object triggered a memory, even the collapsed shed where my brother and I stacked wood each fall. I felt bombarded.

Trees had reclaimed the fields my father cleared. Buildings had fallen in on each other, new roads had appeared and old ones grown over.

That was when it hit me that whenever I visit Kenora, I'm really wanting to travel in time. But the Kenora I miss no longer exists. There are subtle similarities, subtle commonalities with what I remember but that is all.

Some of the wild I carry within remains there. I can still step off the highway and get lost. The wolves, bears, deer, fish, ducks, partridges and other game are still being hunted.

Right up until the end of his life, my father was lucid and continued to tell stories. The last one I remember him telling me was about the man from Chicago who was killed by a black bear. Maybe it was his way of saying he was ready to die.

My mother has lived alone in an apartment these past ten years since my father's death. She is in the beginning stages of Alzheimer's now and some days her memory is good, but on others, I have to remind her who I am when I phone. She hasn't yet forgotten about swimming in Longbow Lake and mentions it now and then, though she never speaks of the three days she hollowed out a place to sleep in the brush along its shore. I'm certain she remembers none of that.

I started this book wanting to call the wild, but got lost in memories instead. My brother still hunts each fall getting a deer or moose, which he puts up for the winter. Until recently, he, like my sister, lived in Winnipeg, but he has moved to Lac Du

Bonnet to be nearer the life he knew as a boy. I've done the same moving to Salt Spring Island. Now each morning when I go for a walk I pass a half-dozen deer grazing along the side of the road. They often look up to take me in but they are not easily spooked even if I yell at them. Hunting deer is illegal on Salt Spring and so they are bountiful and less fearful.

Whenever my father spotted a deer on the side of the highway or in a field near Winnipeg, he lifted his hands as if raising a rifle and then shouted *bang*.

There are eight lakes on Salt Spring Island, and each is carefully charted and completely known. Still I love swimming in their warm waters each summer. They are small lakes, even smaller than Ghost Lake. My brother and I have never talked about Ghost Lake, and until I began this book, I hadn't thought of it in years. Sometimes when I'm in the water and I watch kids roughhousing on the dock and throwing each other in, I sense I haven't traveled as far as I've thought. As I tread water, I could be in any lake, even Ghost Lake, my feet kicking wildly to keep my head above water.

Then there is the story of Chickadee to consider. I suppose like my father claimed he could have been out there in the bush for years, a shadow slipping between the trees, just out of reach, but not that far away. Maybe the wild can call us back. And like my father knew, some stories don't have an ending.

MEMBER OF SCABRINI GROUP

Québec, Canada
2005